Virtually
VEGETARIAN

Styling DONNA HAY
Photography QUENTIN BACON

A J.B. Fairfax Press Publication

INTRODUCTION

Eating less red meat and more fish, chicken, grains, beans and vegetables has become increasingly popular in recent years. This book presents a selection of imaginative recipes for those who consider themselves to be 'almost' or 'virtually' vegetarian.

Many of the dishes that use fish or chicken do so as a secondary ingredient or flavouring rather than the main ingredient and because of this, many of these dishes can easily be adapted to vegetarian by adding more vegetables or by substituting beans, lentils or grains.

EDITORIAL
Food Editor: Rachel Blackmore
Editors: Kirsten John, Linda Venturoni
Editorial and Production Assistant: Danielle Thiris
Editorial Coordinator: Margaret Kelly
UK Food Consultant: Katie Swallow

Photography: Quentin Bacon
Styling and Food: Donna Hay
Home Economist and Recipe Development: Jody Vassallo
Illustrated Backgrounds: Angela Konieczny

DESIGN AND PRODUCTION
Manager: Sheridan Carter
Layout and Design: Lulu Dougherty
Senior Production Editor: Anna Maguire
Production Editor: Sheridan Packer
Cover Design: Michele Withers
Chapter Openers: Susan Griffiths

Published by J.B. Fairfax Press Pty Limited
80-82 McLachlan Avenue
Rushcutters Bay, NSW 2011, Australia
A.C.N. 003 738 430

Formatted by J.B. Fairfax Press Pty Limited
Printed by Toppan Printing Co., Hong Kong
PRINTED IN HONG KONG

JBFP 347
Includes Index
ISBN 1 86343 185 3

DISTRIBUTION AND SALES
Australia: J.B. Fairfax Press Pty Limited
Ph: (02) 361 6366 Fax: (02) 360 6262
United Kingdom: J.B. Fairfax Press Limited
Ph: (0933) 402330 Fax: (0933) 402234

ABOUT THIS BOOK

INGREDIENTS

Unless otherwise stated the following ingredients are used in this book:

Cream — Double, suitable for whipping
Flour — White flour, plain or standard
Sugar — White sugar

WHAT'S IN A TABLESPOON?

AUSTRALIA
1 tablespoon = 20 mL or 4 teaspoons
NEW ZEALAND
1 tablespoon = 15 mL or 3 teaspoons
UNITED KINGDOM
1 tablespoon = 15 mL or 3 teaspoons
The recipes in this book were tested in Australia where a 20 mL tablespoon is standard. The tablespoon in the New Zealand and the United Kingdom sets of measuring spoons is 15 mL. For recipes using baking powder, gelatine, bicarbonate of soda, small quantities of flour and cornflour, simply add another teaspoon for each tablespoon specified.

CANNED FOODS

Can sizes vary between countries and manufacturers. You may find the quantities in this book are slightly different to what is available. Purchase and use the can size nearest to the suggested size in the recipe.

MICROWAVE IT

Where microwave instructions occur in this book, a microwave oven with a 650 watt output has been used. Wattage on domestic microwave ovens varies between 500 and 700 watts, so it may be necessary to vary cooking times slightly depending on the wattage of your oven.

CONTENTS

FAST FEASTS

*Dip into this chapter
to create tasty treats
in a flash.
All of them take less
than 30 minutes
to make and maximise
the convenience
of quick-cooking grains,
canned fish
and pre-cooked beans.*

ORIENTAL CHICKEN PIZZA
Chicken

Oven temperature
200°C, 400°F, Gas 6

For a complete meal serve this tasty pizza with a selection of your favourite salads.
Sweet soy sauce also known as kechap manis can be used instead of teriyaki in this recipe if you wish.

1 packaged 30 cm/12 in pizza base
$1/4$ cup/60 mL/2 fl oz thick teriyaki sauce
2 boneless chicken breast fillets, cooked and sliced
125 g/4 oz snow peas (mangetout), thinly sliced
4 spring onions, sliced
155 g/5 oz tofu, chopped
6 asparagus spears, cut into 5 cm/2 in pieces
3 tablespoons chopped fresh coriander
3 tablespoons sesame seeds, toasted
2 tablespoons sweet chilli sauce

1 Place pizza base on a lightly greased baking tray. Spread base with teriyaki sauce and top with chicken, snow peas (mangetout), spring onions, tofu and asparagus. Sprinkle with coriander and sesame seeds.

2 Drizzle chilli sauce over pizza and bake for 30 minutes or until base is golden and crisp.

Serves 4

SPICY TOFU AND BEAN NACHOS
Vegetarian

Oven temperature
200°C, 400°F, Gas 6

Tofu is very high in protein (7.8 per cent), an excellent source of calcium and a good source of iron, phosphorus and B-complex vitamins. Marinated tofu is available in packets from health food stores and some supermarkets.

250 g/8 oz corn chips
315 g/10 oz bottled spicy tomato salsa
155 g/5 oz marinated tofu, chopped
440 g/14 oz canned red kidney beans, rinsed and drained
3 spring onions, sliced
1 red pepper, thinly sliced
185 g/6 oz grated tasty cheese (mature Cheddar)
$1/4$ cup/45 g/$1^1/_2$ oz natural yogurt

1 Divide corn chips between four shallow heatproof bowls. Top each bowl with equal amounts of salsa, tofu, red kidney beans, spring onions and red pepper.

2 Sprinkle with cheese and bake for 20 minutes or until cheese melts and is golden.

3 Top each bowl with a spoonful of yogurt and serve immediately.

Serves 4

Previous page: Oriental Chicken Pizza,
Chicken and Avocado Focaccia
Right: Spicy Tofu and Bean Nachos

CHICKEN AND AVOCADO FOCACCIA
Chicken

2 teaspoons vegetable oil
2 boneless chicken breast fillets, sliced
1 teaspoon paprika
1 teaspoon ground cumin
4 x 12 cm/5 in focaccia squares, split and toasted
4 slices Swiss cheese
$^1/_2$ cucumber, sliced

AVOCADO SALSA
1 avocado, stoned, peeled and mashed
2 tablespoons chopped fresh coriander
2 tablespoons lime or lemon juice
2 tablespoons mayonnaise
1 fresh red chilli, chopped

1   To make salsa, place avocado, coriander, lime or lemon juice, mayonnaise and chilli in a bowl and mix gently to combine. Set aside.

2   Heat oil in a frying pan over a medium heat, add chicken, paprika and cumin and cook, stirring, for 5 minutes or until chicken is tender.

3   Top focaccia bases with chicken mixture, cheese and cucumber. Spoon over salsa and top with remaining focaccia halves. Serve immediately.

Serves 4

A combination of chopped fresh chives and mint may be used instead of the coriander.

CHILLI BEAN ROLLS
Vegetarian

315 g/10 oz prepared puff pastry
1 egg, lightly beaten

CHILLI BEAN FILLING
440 g/14 oz canned red kidney beans,
rinsed and drained
4 tablespoons tomato paste (purée)
2 tablespoons mild chilli sauce
60 g/2 oz grated tasty cheese
(mature Cheddar)
1 teaspoon ground cumin
1 teaspoon ground coriander

Serve these tasty rolls with chilli or tomato sauce or a dip as an appetiser or, accompanied by a crisp salad, as a starter or light luncheon dish.

Makes 8

1   Roll out pastry to 3 mm/^{1}/8 in thick and cut into eight 10 x 15 cm/4 in x 6 in rectangles. Set aside.

2   To make filling, place red kidney beans, tomato paste (purée), chilli sauce, cheese, cumin and coriander in a bowl. Mash lightly to combine.

3   Place a spoonful of filling lengthwise down the centre of each pastry rectangle. Fold edges over and roll to encase filling.

4   Place rolls on greased baking trays, brush with egg and bake for 20 minutes or until pastry is puffed and golden.

POTATO CAKE STACKS

Fish or Vegetarian

Left: Chilli Bean Rolls
Above: Potato Cake Stacks

3 potatoes, grated
3 tablespoons snipped fresh chives
2 tablespoons flour
$^1/_4$ cup/45 g/1$^1/_2$ oz natural yogurt
1 egg, lightly beaten
30 g/1 oz butter

SOUR CREAM FILLING
$^1/_2$ cup/125 g/4 oz sour cream
$^1/_2$ cup/60 g/2 oz grated tasty cheese
(mature Cheddar)
220 g/7 oz canned tuna, drained and
flaked (optional)
freshly ground black pepper

Serves 4

1   To make filling, combine sour cream, cheese, tuna (if using) and black pepper to taste in a bowl. Set aside.

2   Place potatoes, chives, flour, yogurt and egg in a bowl and mix to combine.

3   Melt butter in a frying pan over a medium heat. Add tablespoons of potato mixture, flatten with an egg slice and cook for 2 minutes each side or until golden. Remove from pan, set aside and keep warm and repeat to use remaining mixture.

4   To serve, top half the potato cakes with a spoon of filling, then with remaining potato cakes.

Canned salmon or chopped cooked chicken are delicious alternatives to the tuna in this recipe.

11

CHICKPEA AND TOMATO CURRY

Vegetarian

Made from fresh red chillies, red curry paste lends distinctive colour to Malaysian-style curries. If you prefer, substitute green curry paste (prepared from green chillies) or any of the many varieties of curry pastes available from gourmet or international sections of supermarkets and in Oriental food stores.

1 tablespoon vegetable oil
1 clove garlic, crushed
2 tablespoons finely grated fresh ginger
1 onion, chopped
1 tablespoon ground cumin
1 tablespoon ground coriander
1 tablespoon red curry paste
440 g/14 oz canned tomatoes, undrained and mashed
440 g/14 oz canned chickpeas, rinsed and drained
125 g/4 oz button mushrooms, halved
3 hard-boiled eggs, quartered
3 tablespoons chopped fresh mint
freshly ground black pepper
60 g/2 oz shredded coconut, toasted

1 Heat oil in a large saucepan over a medium heat, add garlic, ginger and onion and cook, stirring, for 3 minutes or until onion is golden. Add cumin, coriander and curry paste and cook for 2 minutes longer.

2 Add tomatoes and chickpeas and bring to the boil. Reduce heat and simmer for 10 minutes.

3 Stir in mushrooms, eggs and mint and cook for 3 minutes or until curry is heated through. Season to taste with black pepper, sprinkle with coconut and serve immediately.

Serves 4

PEANUT NOODLES

Fish or Vegetarian

Soba noodles are made from finely ground buckwheat flour and packaged as dried, straight flat sticks about 25 cm/10 in long. They are available from Oriental food stores. Substitute with wholewheat noodles, if you prefer.

500 g/1 lb soba noodles
1 tablespoon sesame oil
4 spring onions, chopped
185 g/6 oz snow peas (mangetout), sliced
1 red pepper, sliced
185 g/6 oz uncooked prawns, shelled and deveined (optional)
220 g/7 oz dry roasted peanuts
2 tablespoons chopped fresh coriander
2 tablespoons balsamic or red wine vinegar

1 Cook noodles in boiling water in a large saucepan following packet directions or until tender. Drain, set aside and keep warm.

2 Heat oil in a wok or large frying pan over a high heat, add spring onions, snow peas (mangetout), red pepper and prawns (if using) and stir-fry for 5 minutes or until prawns are just cooked.

3 Add noodles, peanuts, coriander and vinegar to pan and toss well to combine. Stir-fry for 4 minutes longer or until heated through. Serve immediately.

Serves 4

Peanut Noodles, Chickpea and Tomato Curry

Plate Accoutrement

SOY BURGERS
Vegetarian

6 multigrain rolls, split and toasted
6 lettuce leaves of your choice
30 g/1 oz alfalfa sprouts
2 large tomatoes, sliced
1 raw beetroot, grated
4 tablespoons sunflower seeds, toasted

MINTED SOY BURGERS
440 g/14 oz canned soy beans, rinsed and drained
1 cup/60 g/2 oz wholemeal breadcrumbs, made from stale bread
1 red onion, finely chopped
1 carrot, grated
3 tablespoons besan flour
3 tablespoons chopped fresh mint
1 tablespoon finely grated fresh ginger
1 egg, lightly beaten
75 g/2^1/2 oz sesame seeds
2 tablespoons vegetable oil

CREAMY DRESSING
1 cup/200 g/6^1/2 oz natural yogurt
1 tablespoon chopped fresh coriander
1 tablespoon grated fresh ginger
2 tablespoons sweet chilli sauce
1 clove garlic, crushed
freshly ground black pepper

Besan flour is made from chickpeas and is available from Asian and health food stores (you can substitute pea flour made from split peas, if desired). To make your own besan flour, place chickpeas on a baking tray and bake at 180°C/350°F/Gas 4 for 15-20 minutes or until roasted. Cool, then using a food processor or blender grind to make a fine flour.

1 To make dressing, place yogurt, coriander, ginger, chilli sauce, garlic and black pepper to taste in a bowl and mix to combine.

2 To make burgers, place soy beans in a food processor or blender and process to roughly chop. Place chopped beans, breadcrumbs, onion, carrot, flour, mint, ginger and egg in a bowl and mix well to combine. Shape mixture into six burgers and roll each in sesame seeds.

3 Heat oil in a frying pan over a medium heat, add burgers and cook for 6 minutes each side or until heated through and golden.

4 Top bottom half of each roll with a lettuce leaf, a burger, a few alfalfa sprouts, tomato slices, beetroot, sunflower seeds, a spoonful of dressing and top half of roll. Serve immediately.

Serves 6

Plate Limoges Australia

Soy Burgers

TUNA PANCAKES WITH CORN SALSA

Fish

Tuna Pancakes with Corn Salsa

PANCAKES

1 cup/155 g/5 oz wholemeal flour
2 eggs, lightly beaten
³/4 cup/185 mL/6 fl oz soy milk
1 carrot, grated
1 zucchini (courgette), grated
220 g/7 oz canned tuna, drained and flaked
2 teaspoons chopped fresh lemon thyme or 1 teaspoon dried thyme
freshly ground black pepper
45 g/1¹/2 oz butter, melted

CORN SALSA

1 avocado, stoned, peeled and sliced
125 g/4 oz canned sweet corn kernels, drained
2 spring onions, sliced
1 tomato, chopped
1 tablespoon lime or lemon juice
1 fresh red chilli, chopped

Serves 4

1 To make pancakes, place flour in a bowl. Add eggs and milk and mix until smooth. Stir in carrot, zucchini (courgette), tuna, thyme and black pepper to taste.

2 Melt butter in a frying pan over a medium heat, add 2 tablespoons of mixture to pan and cook for 1-2 minutes or until bubbles form on the surface, then turn and cook for 1-2 minutes longer or until golden. Remove from pan, set aside and keep warm. Repeat with remaining mixture to make 12 pancakes.

3 To make salsa, combine avocado, sweet corn, spring onions, tomato, lime or lemon juice and chilli in a bowl.

4 To serve, place three pancakes on each serving plate and top generously with salsa.

Oily fish such as tuna and salmon are rich in Omega-3 fats which are now believed to protect the heart against disease by lowering blood pressure and reducing fatty build-up on blood vessel walls. Omega-3 fats are said to reduce the tendency for the blood to clot and so lessen its 'stickiness'.

RITZY RICE
AND
OTHER GRAINS

*Rice and grains
have long been versatile
partners on any plate.*

*In this chapter
they take centre stage
in delicious salads, tasty
bakes and pilaus.*

*Here you find inspiring
ideas not only for rice
but also for newcomers
such as couscous,
corn meal (polenta)
and wild rice.*

WARM RICE AND MUSHROOM SALAD
Chicken or Vegetarian

The rice for this recipe is best cooked just prior to assembling the salad. If the rice has been cooked in advance reheat it in the microwave.

45 g/1¹/2 oz butter
2 boneless chicken breast fillets, sliced (optional)
125 g/4 oz snow peas (mangetout)
125 g/4 oz oyster mushrooms
125 g/4 oz button mushrooms
2 tablespoons chopped fresh lemon thyme or 1 teaspoon dried thyme
1 cup/220 g/7 oz brown rice, cooked
1 cup/220 g/7 oz wild rice, cooked
125 g/4 oz tofu, sliced and fried
4 spring onions, sliced
2 oranges, segmented
3 tablespoons chopped fresh coriander
3 tablespoons pine nuts, toasted

TANGY ORANGE DRESSING
1 tablespoon sesame oil
1 clove garlic, crushed
1 tablespoon grated fresh ginger
1/4 cup/60 mL/2 fl oz orange juice
1 tablespoon honey
1 tablespoon reduced-salt soy sauce
freshly ground black pepper

1 Melt butter in a frying pan over a medium heat, add chicken (if using) and stir-fry for 4 minutes or until chicken is just tender. Add snow peas (mangetout), oyster and button mushrooms and thyme and stir-fry for 3 minutes or until vegetables are tender. Cool slightly.

2 Place rice, vegetable mixture, tofu, spring onions, oranges, coriander and pine nuts in a salad bowl. Toss to combine.

3 To make dressing, heat sesame oil in a small saucepan over a medium heat, add garlic and ginger and stir-fry for 2 minutes or until garlic is just golden. Add orange juice, honey and soy sauce and bring to the boil. Reduce heat and simmer for 5 minutes. Set aside to cool slightly. Season to taste with black pepper. Pour warm dressing over salad. Toss to combine.

Serves 4

Before frying tofu, remove any excess moisture by wrapping tofu in a clean teatowel and placing under a weighted dinner plate for 15-30 minutes. Slice tofu and fry in vegetable oil.

RICE AND CHEESE TRIANGLES
Vegetarian

Oven temperature
180°C, 350°F, Gas 4

30 g/1 oz butter
2 cups/440 g/14 oz Arborio or risotto rice
4 cups/1 litre/1³/4 pt hot vegetable stock
freshly ground black pepper

GORGONZOLA TOPPING
185 g/6 oz gorgonzola or soft blue cheese
1/2 cup/125 g/4 oz sour cream
3 tablespoons snipped fresh chives

1 Melt butter in a saucepan over a medium heat, add rice and cook, stirring constantly, for 4 minutes or until rice is translucent. Add 1 cup/250 mL/8 fl oz hot stock and cook, stirring constantly, until liquid is absorbed. Continue cooking in this way until all the stock is used and rice is a thick mixture that sticks together. Season to taste with black pepper. Spread rice mixture over the base of a greased 26 x 32 cm/10¹/2 x 12³/4 in Swiss roll tin.

2 To make topping, place gorgonzola or blue cheese, sour cream and chives in a bowl and mix to combine. Spread topping over rice and bake for 20 minutes or until firm and golden. To serve, cut into large triangles.

Any creamy blue vein cheese can be used to make this delicious dish. Serve with a tossed green salad and crusty bread.

*Previous page: Asparagus Rice Tart, Warm Rice and Mushroom Salad
Right: Rice and Cheese Triangles*

Serves 4

ASPARAGUS RICE TART
Vegetarian

RICE CRUST
1 cup/220 g/7 oz brown rice, cooked
125 g/4 oz grated tasty cheese (mature Cheddar)
30 g/1 oz butter, melted
2 tablespoons snipped fresh chives
2 eggs, lightly beaten

ASPARAGUS FILLING
2 teaspoons vegetable oil
2 onions, chopped
440 g/14 oz asparagus spears, cut into 5 cm/2 in pieces
1 red pepper, sliced
125 g/4 oz snow peas (mangetout), sliced
5 eggs, lightly beaten
1 cup/250 g/8 oz sour cream
30 g/1 oz grated Parmesan cheese
freshly ground black pepper

1   To make crust, place rice, cheese, butter, chives and 2 eggs in a bowl and mix well to combine. Press mixture over the base and up the sides of a greased deep-sided 23 cm/9 in flan tin. Set aside.

2   To make filling, heat oil in a frying pan over a medium heat, add onions and cook, stirring, for 5 minutes or until onions are soft and golden. Add asparagus, red pepper and snow peas (mangetout) and cook for 3 minutes longer. Remove pan from heat and set aside to cool completely.

3   Place 5 eggs, sour cream, Parmesan cheese and black pepper to taste in a bowl and mix to combine. Stir in asparagus mixture. Pour filling into rice crust and bake for 1 hour or until filling is set.

Serves 4-6

Oven temperature
160°C, 325°F, Gas 3

Toasted sesame seeds make a deliciously nutty addition to the rice crust. When fresh asparagus is unavailable, use another green vegetable such as broccoli, Brussels sprouts or green beans.

Plate Limoges Australia

Above: Saffron and Chicken Risotto
Right: Rice Noodle Pancakes

SAFFRON AND CHICKEN RISOTTO

Chicken

4 cups/1 litre/1³/₄ pt vegetable stock
1 cup/250 mL/8 fl oz dry white wine
1 tablespoon vegetable oil
2 boneless chicken breast fillets, sliced
45 g/1¹/₂ oz butter
3 leeks, sliced
2 cups/440 g/14 oz Arborio or
risotto rice
pinch saffron threads
60 g/2 oz grated Parmesan cheese
freshly ground black pepper

Arborio rice is traditionally used for making risottos, as it absorbs liquid without becoming soft. If Arborio rice is unavailable, substitute with any short grain rice. A risotto made in the traditional way, where liquid is added a little at a time as the rice cooks, will take 20-30 minutes to cook.

1   Place stock and wine in a saucepan and bring to the boil over a medium heat. Reduce heat and keep warm.

2   Heat oil in a saucepan over a medium heat, add chicken and cook, stirring, for 5 minutes or until chicken is tender. Remove chicken from pan and set aside.

3   Add butter and leeks to same pan and cook over a low heat, stirring, for 8 minutes or until leeks are golden and caramelised.

4   Add rice and saffron to pan and cook over a medium heat, stirring constantly, for 3 minutes or until rice becomes translucent. Pour 1 cup/250 mL/8 fl oz hot stock mixture into rice mixture and cook, stirring constantly, until liquid is absorbed. Continue cooking in this way until all the stock is used and rice is tender.

5   Stir chicken, Parmesan cheese and black pepper to taste into rice mixture and cook for 2 minutes longer. Serve immediately.

Serves 4

RICE NOODLE PANCAKES
Vegetarian

220 g/7 oz rice noodles
vegetable oil, for shallow frying
60 g/2 oz roasted cashews

VEGETABLE TOPPING
2 tablespoons olive oil
10 baby eggplant (aubergines), sliced
lengthwise
1 tablespoon sesame oil
1 clove garlic, crushed
2 small fresh red chillies, sliced
6 spring onions, sliced diagonally
2 carrots, cut into thin strips
$^1/_2$ cup/125 mL/4 fl oz reduced-salt
soy sauce
$1^1/_2$ tablespoons rice wine vinegar
$^1/_4$ cup/45 g/$1^1/_2$ oz brown sugar

1   To make topping, heat olive oil in a frying pan over a medium heat and cook eggplant (aubergine) slices, turning frequently, for 5 minutes or until soft. Drain on absorbent kitchen paper. Heat sesame oil in same pan, add garlic, chillies, spring onions and carrots and stir-fry for 5 minutes or carrots are just tender. Remove from pan and set aside.

2   Add soy sauce, vinegar and sugar to pan and bring to the boil. Reduce heat and simmer for 5 minutes or until sugar dissolves and mixture thickens. Add eggplant (aubergines) and carrot mixture and simmer for 3 minutes. Keep warm.

3   Cook noodles following packet directions. Drain and dry on absorbent kitchen paper. Divide noodles into six portions. Heat vegetable oil in frying pan over a medium heat. Add noodle portions, one at a time, flatten with a spatula and cook for 4 minutes each side or until golden and crisp. Drain on absorbent kitchen paper. Top each pancake with some topping and sprinkle with cashews.

Serves 6

Also known as rice vermicelli or rice sticks, rice noodles vary in size from a very narrow vermicelli style to a ribbon noodle about 5 mm/$^1/_4$ in wide. Before cooking, soak the narrow noodles in cold water for about 10 minutes and the wider ones, about 30 minutes. Once soaked, these noodles take just 2-3 minutes to cook.

Plate Limoges Australia

MEDITERRANEAN SALAD
Fish or Vegetarian

Couscous is a cracked wheat product made from the endosperm of durum wheat and, like bulghur wheat, is very versatile and quick to prepare. After soaking in water, mix couscous with salad ingredients and serve cold; toss with dried fruits, seeds and nuts and serve as a pilau or simply serve hot with milk and fresh fruit as a breakfast 'porridge'.

185 g/6 oz couscous
2 cups/500 mL/16 fl oz boiling water
1 tablespoon olive oil
1 tablespoon balsamic vinegar
freshly ground black pepper
1 cucumber, sliced
1 green pepper, chopped
3 plum (egg or Italian) tomatoes, chopped
12 sun-dried tomatoes, sliced
60 g/2 oz marinated artichokes, drained and sliced
60 g/2 oz pitted black olives, sliced
185 g/6 oz cooked prawns, shelled and deveined (optional)
125 g/4 oz feta cheese, cut into 2 cm/³/4 in cubes
2 tablespoons chopped fresh basil or 2 teaspoons dried basil
2 teaspoons finely grated lime or lemon rind

1   Place couscous in a bowl, pour over boiling water and toss with a fork until couscous absorbs all the liquid. Add oil, vinegar and black pepper to taste and toss to combine. Set aside.

2   Place cucumber, green pepper, fresh and dried tomatoes, artichokes, olives, prawns (if using), feta cheese, basil and lime or lemon rind in a salad bowl and toss to combine. Add couscous mixture and toss.

Serves 4

Plate Limoges Australia

POLENTA AND CHEESE LOAF
Vegetarian

200 g/6¹/2 oz corn meal (polenta)
3 cups/750 mL/1¹/4 pt vegetable stock
30 g/1 oz butter
60 g/2 oz grated Parmesan cheese
1 tablespoon chopped fresh rosemary or
1 teaspoon dried rosemary
1 red pepper, halved, roasted and skin
removed, thinly sliced
1 green pepper, halved, roasted and skin
removed, thinly sliced
185 g/6 oz goat's cheese, crumbled

Serves 4

1 Place corn meal (polenta) and
1 cup/250 mL/8 fl oz stock in a saucepan
and whisk until smooth. Place pan over a
medium heat and gradually stir in
remaining stock. Cook, stirring
constantly, for 15-20 minutes or until
corn meal (polenta) leaves side of pan.
Stir in butter, Parmesan cheese and
rosemary.

2 Spoon half the polenta mixture into a
greased 11 x 21 cm/4¹/2 x 8¹/2 in loaf tin.
Place red pepper strips lengthwise along
one side of loaf and green pepper strips
along the other side. Arrange goat's
cheese down the centre.

3 Top with remaining polenta mixture
and press firmly with the back of a spoon.
Bake for 20 minutes or until loaf is firm.
Stand loaf in tin for 5 minutes before
turning out.

Left: Mediterranean Salad
Above: Polenta and Cheese Loaf

Oven temperature
180°C, 350°F, Gas 4

Serve this loaf with natural
yogurt flavoured with
chopped fresh herbs.
To roast peppers, halve and
seed peppers and place,
skin side up, under a
preheated hot grill. Cook
until skin blisters and chars,
then place in a paper or
plastic food bag, seal and
set aside until cool enough to
handle. Remove from bag,
peel away skin and discard.
Slice peppers and use as
directed in recipe.

PUNGENT RICE AND LENTIL PILAU
Vegetarian

1 cup/220 g/7 oz long grain rice
200 g/6^1/$_2$ oz green lentils
3 tablespoons vegetable oil
2 teaspoons garam masala
1 teaspoon ground cumin
1 teaspoon ground coriander
3 onions, sliced

1   Bring a large saucepan of water to the boil. Add rice and lentils, reduce heat and simmer for 15 minutes or until rice and lentils are tender. Drain and set aside.

2   Heat 2 teaspoons oil in a frying pan over a medium heat, add garam masala, cumin and coriander and cook, stirring, for 2 minutes. Add rice and lentil mixture and cook, stirring, for 4 minutes longer. Remove pan from heat, set aside and keep warm.

3   Heat remaining oil in a separate frying pan over a medium heat, add onions and cook, stirring, for 6 minutes or until onions are crisp and golden. Sprinkle onions over pilaf. Serve hot, warm or at room temperature.

For a complete meal serve with naan bread.
For something different briefly steam or blanch fresh young spinach leaves until wilted, finely shred and stir into pilau at the end of step 2.

Serves 4

THAI FRIED RICE
Chicken

2 teaspoons vegetable oil
1 teaspoon red curry paste
2 stalks fresh lemon grass, chopped or
1 teaspoon dried lemon grass or
1 teaspoon finely grated lemon rind
2 tablespoons chopped fresh coriander
2 boneless chicken breast fillets, sliced
185 g/6 oz snow peas (mangetout)
1 red pepper, chopped
1 small eggplant (aubergine), chopped
315 g/10 oz jasmine or basmati rice, cooked
3 tablespoons sweet chilli sauce
2 tablespoons sweet soy sauce

1   Heat oil in a wok or large frying pan over a high heat, add curry paste, lemon grass or lemon rind and coriander and stir-fry for 1 minute.

2   Add chicken to pan and stir-fry for 5 minutes or until chicken is just cooked. Add snow peas (mangetout), red pepper and eggplant (aubergine) and stir-fry for 3 minutes longer.

3   Add rice, chilli sauce and soy sauce, toss to combine and stir-fry for 3 minutes or until mixture is heated through.

Jasmine and basmati rice are fragrant long grain rices used in Thai and Indian cooking. 'Basmati' means 'fragrance' in the Indian language and both rices give off a wonderfully distinctive aroma as they cook.

Serves 4

Pungent Rice and Lentil Pilau, Thai Fried Rice

IMAGINATIVE
BEANS
AND
LENTILS

*Beans never tasted
this good!
From tangy salads
to hearty casseroles,
this chapter features
the best of beans
and lentils.
Long regarded as
the centrepiece
of a balanced
vegetarian diet,
beans and lentils
are fast proving
themselves just as tasty
as they are nutritious.*

SPICY CORN AND LENTIL CHOWDER
Chicken

200 g/6^1/$_2$ oz red lentils
30 g/1 oz butter
2 cloves garlic, crushed
1 onion, chopped
1 small fresh green chilli, chopped
1 teaspoon ground cardamom
1 teaspoon ground cumin
2 cups/500 mL/16 fl oz vegetable stock
1^1/$_2$ cups/375 mL/12 fl oz coconut milk
250 g/8 oz cooked chicken, chopped
375 g/12 oz canned creamed sweet corn
3 tablespoons chopped fresh coriander

Serves 6

1 Bring a large saucepan of water to the boil. Add lentils, reduce heat and simmer for 12 minutes or until tender. Drain and set aside.

2 Melt butter in a saucepan over a medium heat, add garlic, onion, chilli, cardamom and cumin and cook, stirring, for 3 minutes or until onion is soft.

3 Add lentils, stock, coconut milk, chicken and sweet corn and bring to the boil. Reduce heat and simmer for 45 minutes. Sprinkle with coriander and serve.

One of the simplest soups you can make for a hearty and economical family meal.

GRILLED CHICKEN WITH LENTIL PUREE
Chicken

2 boneless chicken breast fillets,
halved lengthwise
1 red pepper, quartered
1 green pepper, quartered
2 zucchini (courgettes), halved
lengthwise

LENTIL PUREE
155 g/5 oz green lentils
1^1/$_2$ cups/375 mL/12 fl oz vegetable stock
1 teaspoon garam masala
^{1}/$_2$ teaspoon ground cinnamon
freshly ground black pepper

Serves 4

1 To make purée, bring a large saucepan of water to the boil. Add lentils, reduce heat and simmer for 15 minutes or until tender. Drain and set aside to cool slightly. Place lentils and stock in a food processor or blender and process until smooth.

2 Transfer purée to a saucepan, stir in garam marsala, cinnamon and black pepper to taste and cook over a medium heat, stirring, for 4 minutes or until purée thickens and is heated through. Set aside and keep warm.

3 Cook chicken, red and green peppers and zucchini (courgettes) under a preheated hot grill or on a barbecue, turning several times, for 10 minutes or until cooked and tender. Serve immediately with warm purée.

Recent studies have shown that the fibre in legumes is soluble, and when eaten as part of a low-fat diet, helps to lower blood cholesterol levels and control the glucose levels of diabetics.

Previous page: Spicy Corn and Lentil Chowder,
Grilled Chicken with Lentil Purée
Right: Moroccan Beans

MOROCCAN BEANS
Chicken or Vegetarian

1 tablespoon vegetable oil
1 tablespoon grated fresh ginger
1 teaspoon ground cinnamon
1 teaspoon cumin seeds
$^1/_2$ teaspoon turmeric
2 onions, chopped
440 g/14 oz canned red kidney beans,
rinsed and drained
440 g/14 oz canned soy beans, rinsed
and drained
440 g/14 oz canned chickpeas, rinsed
and drained
375 g/12 oz chopped cooked chicken
(optional)
440 g/14 oz canned tomato paste
(purée)
1 cup/250 mL/8 fl oz vegetable stock
75 g/2$^1/_2$ oz currants
60 g/2 oz pine nuts, toasted

1   Heat oil in a saucepan over a medium heat, add ginger, cinnamon, cumin seeds, and turmeric and cook, stirring, for 1 minute. Add onions and cook for 3 minutes longer or until onions are soft.

2   Add red kidney beans, soy beans, chickpeas, chicken (if using), tomato paste (purée) and stock to pan and bring to the boil. Reduce heat and simmer for 10 minutes.

3   Add currants and pine nuts and cook for 2 minutes longer.

Serves 4-6

For a complete meal, be sure to serve this delicious mix with a hearty wholegrain bread so that all the essential amino acids are present to build complete protein.

KEBABS WITH BROAD BEAN PUREE
Vegetarian

250 g/8 oz cherry tomatoes
155 g/5 oz button mushrooms
3 zucchini (courgettes), cut into thick rounds
1 yellow or green pepper, cut into chunks
250 g/8 oz marinated tofu, cut into 2 cm/^{3}/$_4$ in cubes
1 red pepper, cut into chunks

TANGY CITRUS MARINADE
2 tablespoons lime or lemon juice
2 tablespoons honey
1 tablespoon reduced-salt soy sauce
1 tablespoon vegetable oil

BROAD BEAN PUREE
250 g/8 oz shelled fresh or frozen broad beans
^{1}/$_2$ cup/100 g/3^1/$_2$ oz natural yogurt
1 tablespoon chopped fresh thyme or 1 teaspoon dried thyme
2 teaspoons finely grated orange rind
freshly ground black pepper

1   Thread tomatoes, mushrooms, zucchini (courgettes), yellow or green pepper, tofu and red pepper onto lightly oiled skewers.

2   To make marinade, combine lime or lemon juice, honey, soy sauce and oil. Brush over kebabs and marinate for 1 hour.

3   To make purée, bring a saucepan of water to the boil, add broad beans and cook for 10 minutes or until beans are tender. Drain and cool slightly. Place broad beans, yogurt, thyme, orange rind and black pepper to taste in a food processor or blender and process until smooth. Set aside.

4   Cook kebabs under a preheated hot grill, turning frequently, for 8 minutes or until tender. Serve with purée.

Serves 4

Any cooked or canned beans can be used in this purée when broad beans are not available.

Plate Limoges Australia

Left: Kebabs with Broad Bean Purée
Above: Salmon and Lentil Salad

SALMON AND LENTIL SALAD

Fish

1 cos lettuce, leaves separated and torn
into large pieces
200 g/6$^{1}/_{2}$ oz green lentils, cooked and
drained
200 g/6$^{1}/_{2}$ oz red lentils, cooked and
drained
250 g/8 oz cherry tomatoes, halved
155 g/5 oz prepared wholemeal croûtons
1 tablespoon chilli oil or vegetable oil
375 g/12 oz salmon fillets, skin and
bones removed, cut into 3 cm/1$^{1}/_{4}$ in
wide strips
fresh Parmesan cheese
freshly ground black pepper

CREAMY DRESSING
$^{1}/_{2}$ cup/125 mL/4 fl oz mayonnaise
2 tablespoons vegetable stock
1 tablespoon wholegrain mustard
1 tablespoon white wine vinegar

1   To make dressing, place mayonnaise,
stock, mustard and vinegar in a bowl and
mix to combine. Set aside.

2   Arrange lettuce, cooked lentils,
tomatoes and croûtons attractively on a
serving platter. Set aside.

3   Heat oil in a frying pan over a medium
heat, add salmon and cook, turning
several times, for 4 minutes or until
salmon is cooked. Remove from pan and
arrange on top of salad. Drizzle dressing
over salad and top with shavings of
Parmesan cheese and black pepper to
taste.

Serves 4

The iron content of legumes
such as lentils is fairly high,
but as it occurs in an
inorganic form, the human
body needs help to absorb it.
You can increase the body's
ability to absorb the iron if
you serve a Vitamin C-rich
food (such as the salad and
tomatoes here) as part of the
same meal.
Use a vegetable peeler or a
coarse grater to make
shavings from a piece of
fresh Parmesan cheese.

LENTIL AND CHEESE LOAF
Fish or Vegetarian

Oven temperature
180°C, 350°F, Gas 4

Quick and easy to prepare, lentils need little or no soaking before cooking. Available in a rainbow of colours – brown, green, red (or orange), yellow and black, this versatile food is equally at home as an accompaniment, or as part of a casserole or salad. The smaller yellow and red lentils purée easily and are a useful addition to soups, while larger varieties retain their shape well after cooking.

155 g/5 oz red lentils
125 g/4 oz grated tasty cheese (mature Cheddar)
220 g/7 oz canned salmon, drained and flaked (optional)
4 spring onions, sliced
3 tablespoons chopped fresh parsley
1 tablespoon lemon juice
1 teaspoon paprika
1 egg, lightly beaten
$^1/_4$ cup/60 mL/2 fl oz cream (double)

SUN-DRIED TOMATO DRESSING
$^1/_2$ cup/125 mL/4 fl oz mayonnaise
6 sun-dried tomatoes, chopped
1 tablespoon chopped fresh basil
freshly ground black pepper

1 Bring a large saucepan of water to the boil. Add lentils, reduce heat and simmer for 20 minutes or until tender. Drain.

2 Place lentils, cheese, salmon (if using), spring onions, parsley, lemon juice, paprika, egg and cream in a bowl and mix well to combine. Spoon mixture into a greased 11 x 21 cm/4$^1/_2$ x 8$^1/_2$ in loaf tin and bake for 40 minutes or until firm.

3 To make dressing, place mayonnaise, sun-dried tomatoes, basil and black pepper to taste in a food processor or blender and process until well combined. Serve with loaf.

Serves 4

LENTIL FRITTATA
Fish or Vegetarian

155 g/5 oz red lentils
2 teaspoons vegetable oil
2 leeks, chopped
20 English spinach leaves, shredded
6 zucchini (courgettes), sliced
220 g/7 oz smoked cod or haddock, cooked and flesh flaked (optional)
6 eggs, lightly beaten
$^3/_4$ cup/155 g/5 oz natural yogurt
2 tablespoons chopped fresh chervil or parsley
freshly ground black pepper

1 Bring a large saucepan of water to the boil. Add lentils, reduce heat and simmer for 20 minutes or until tender. Drain and set aside.

2 Heat oil in a frying pan over a medium heat, add leeks and cook, stirring, for 4 minutes or until soft and golden. Add spinach, zucchini (courgettes) and smoked fish (if using) and cook for 3 minutes longer. Stir in lentils and mix to combine.

3 Place eggs, yogurt, chervil or parsley and black pepper to taste in a bowl and whisk to combine. Pour egg mixture over vegetables in pan and cook over a low heat for 6 minutes or until frittata is almost set. Place pan under a preheated hot grill and cook for 2 minutes or until top is golden.

Don't be limited by the vegetables suggested in this recipe. A frittata is designed to use all kinds of fresh – and leftover cooked – vegetables, so choose the ones you like most from what is available.

Serves 4

Plates Limoges Australia

Lentil and Cheese Loaf, Lentil Frittata

Bowl/ Accoutrement

Above: Hearty Bean Casserole
Right: Chickpea and Trout Salad

All types of beans adapt to a huge range of seasonings. The beans in this casserole can be altered to accommodate whatever you have available.
As an alternative, try a combination of haricot and butter beans with chickpeas, and substitute your favourite spices or dried herbs for the ground cumin and oregano.

HEARTY BEAN CASSEROLE
Vegetarian

155 g/5 oz dried red kidney beans
155 g/5 oz dried black-eyed beans
1 tablespoon vegetable oil
2 cloves garlic, crushed
1 red onion, chopped
440 g/14 oz canned peeled tomatoes, undrained and mashed
1 tablespoon ground cumin
1 tablespoon dry mustard
2 tablespoons golden syrup
1 tablespoon tomato paste (purée)
2 carrots, thickly sliced
3 zucchini (courgettes), thickly sliced
440 g/14 oz canned butter beans, rinsed and drained
100 g/3$^{1}/_{2}$ oz shelled fresh or frozen broad beans
2 tablespoons chopped fresh oregano or 1 teaspoon dried oregano

1 Place red kidney and black-eyed beans in a large bowl, cover with water and set aside to soak overnight. Drain. Bring a large saucepan of water to the boil, add beans and boil for 10 minutes. Reduce heat and simmer for 1 hour or until beans are tender. Drain and set aside.

2 Heat oil in a large saucepan over a medium heat, add garlic and onion and cook, stirring, for 3 minutes or until onion is soft and golden. Add tomatoes, cumin, mustard, golden syrup and tomato paste (purée) and bring to the boil. Reduce heat and simmer for 5 minutes.

3 Add cooked beans, carrots, zucchini (courgettes), butter beans, broad beans and oregano to pan and simmer for 30 minutes or until vegetables are tender.

Serves 4

34

CHICKPEA AND TROUT SALAD
Fish

1 bunch curly endive, leaves separated
1 bunch rocket
440 g/14 oz canned chickpeas, rinsed and drained
125 g/4 oz herbed goat's cheese, crumbled
1 red onion, sliced
250 g/8 oz smoked trout, skin and bones removed, flesh flaked
2 tablespoons chopped fresh basil
1 red pepper, halved, roasted, skin removed and sliced

HONEY LIME DRESSING
$^1/_2$ cup/100 g/3$^1/_2$ oz natural yogurt
1 tablespoon chopped fresh mint
1 tablespoon ground cumin
1 tablespoon honey
1 tablespoon lime juice

1   Arrange endive and rocket on a serving platter. Top with chickpeas, goat's cheese, onion and trout. Sprinkle salad with basil and top with red pepper.

2   To make dressing, place yogurt, mint, cumin, honey and lime juice in a bowl and mix to combine. Drizzle dressing over salad and serve immediately.

Serves 4

Chickpeas are slightly crunchy and lend a nutty flavour to salads like this as well as casseroles, soups and other savoury dishes. Dried chickpeas can be used rather than canned if you wish. To cook chickpeas, soak overnight in cold water. Drain. Place in a large saucepan, cover with cold water and bring to the boil over a medium heat. Reduce heat and simmer for 45-60 minutes or until chickpeas are tender. Drain and cool.

PERFECT PIES
AND
PASTRIES

*Pies and pastries
are all-time
family favourites.
Just as happy
on a summer picnic
blanket as beside
a roaring fire,
this selection
of delicious home bakes
is guaranteed
to warm any occasion.*

INDIVIDUAL ANTIPASTO TARTS
Vegetarian

Oven temperature
180°C, 350°F, Gas 4

375 g/12 oz prepared puff pastry
1 large eggplant (aubergine),
sliced crosswise
salt
2 tablespoons vegetable oil
1 large red pepper, roasted and skin
removed, thinly sliced
125 g/4 oz marinated artichokes, drained
and sliced
125 g/4 oz mozzarella cheese, sliced
1 tablespoon chopped fresh basil
freshly ground black pepper

1   Roll out pastry to 3 mm/^{1}/8 in thick
and cut out four 15 cm/6 in circles. Place
pastry circles on a greased baking tray and
bake for 10 minutes or until pastry is
puffed and golden. Set aside to cool.

2   Place eggplant (aubergine) slices
in a colander set over a bowl and
sprinkle with salt. Set aside to stand for
10 minutes. Rinse eggplant (aubergine)
slices under cold running water and pat
dry with absorbent kitchen paper. Brush
with oil and cook under a preheated hot
grill for 4-5 minutes each side or until
golden.

3   To assemble tarts, top pastry circles
with eggplant (aubergine), red pepper,
artichokes and mozzarella cheese.
Sprinkle with basil and black pepper to
taste. Cook under a preheated hot grill
for 3-4 minutes or until cheese melts.
Serve immediately.

Serves 4

To roast peppers see hint on
page 23.

WILD MUSHROOM AND ONION TART
Fish

Oven temperature
200°C, 400°F, Gas 6

250 g/8 oz prepared puff pastry
1 egg yolk
125 g/4 oz ricotta cheese
1 tablespoon chopped fresh thyme or
1 teaspoon dried thyme
60 g/2 oz butter
3 onions, sliced
3 large flat mushrooms, sliced
125 g/4 oz button mushrooms, sliced
125 g/4 oz oyster mushrooms
125 g/4 oz fresh shiitake mushrooms
185 g/6 oz smoked trout, bones and skin
removed, flesh flaked
freshly ground black pepper

1   Roll out pastry to form a 25 x 30 cm/
10 x 12 in rectangle. Place pastry
rectangle on a greased baking tray and
brush with egg yolk.

2   Combine ricotta cheese and thyme
and spread over pastry leaving a
2 cm/^{3}/4 in border. Set aside.

3   Melt 30 g/1 oz butter in a saucepan
over a medium heat, add onions and
cook, stirring, for 10 minutes or until
onions are soft and caramelised. Scatter
onions over cheese.

4   Melt remaining butter in saucepan
over a medium heat, add flat, button,
oyster and shiitake mushrooms and cook,
stirring, for 5 minutes or until mushrooms
are soft. Scatter mushrooms over onions,
top with trout and season to taste with
black pepper. Bake for 30 minutes or
until pastry is puffed and golden.

The flavours and textures
offered by combining
different mushrooms in this
recipe make it an interesting
first course for a dinner party.
You can use any
combination of fresh
mushrooms to make this tart.

Serves 4-6

ALL-TIME VEGETABLE PIE

Vegetarian

125 g/4 oz grated tasty cheese
(mature Cheddar)
1 cup/60 g/2 oz breadcrumbs, made
from stale bread

PASTRY
1¹/₂ cups/185 g/6 oz flour
90 g/3 oz butter
1 egg, lightly beaten
1-2 tablespoons iced water

VEGETABLE FILLING
1 tablespoon vegetable oil
1 onion, sliced
2 leeks, sliced
250 g/8 oz pumpkin flesh, chopped
2 potatoes, chopped
¹/₄ cauliflower, broken into
small florets
1 parsnip, chopped
1 small head broccoli, broken into
small florets
1 red pepper, chopped
125 g/4 oz frozen peas
¹/₂ cup/125 mL/4 fl oz vegetable stock
2 tablespoons chopped fresh basil

1 To make pastry, place flour and butter in a food processor and process until mixture resembles fine breadcrumbs. With machine running, slowly add egg and enough water to form a soft dough. Turn dough onto a lightly floured surface and knead briefly. Wrap dough in plastic food wrap and refrigerate for 30 minutes.

2 Roll out pastry to fit a deep 23 cm/9 in flan tin with a removable base. Line pastry case with nonstick baking paper, fill with uncooked rice and bake for 10 minutes. Remove rice and paper and bake for 10 minutes longer or until pastry is golden and crisp. Set aside to cool.

3 To make filling, heat oil in a large frying pan over a medium heat, add onion and leeks and cook, stirring, for 4 minutes or until onion is golden. Add pumpkin and potatoes and cook, stirring, for 10 minutes longer or until potatoes are just tender.

4 Add cauliflower, parsnip, broccoli, red pepper, peas and stock to pan and bring to the boil. Reduce heat and simmer for 10 minutes or until vegetables are soft. Mix in basil. Set aside to cool.

5 Spoon cold filling into pastry case. Combine cheese and breadcrumbs, sprinkle over filling and bake for 20 minutes or until top is golden.

Serves 6

Oven temperature
180°C, 350°F, Gas 4

If preferred, use wholemeal plain flour to prepare a pastry with a nuttier flavour. Alternatively, when you're in a hurry, a quick pie shell can be prepared with four sheets of filo pastry layered together with melted margarine or oil and trimmed to fit the flan tin.

Plate Accoutrement

*Previous page: All-time Vegetable Pie,
Individual Antipasto Tarts
Right: Wild Mushroom and Onion Tart*

TWO POTATO PIE
Vegetarian

Oven temperature
180°C, 350°F, Gas 4

Warm or cold, this pie makes
a perfect picnic lunch and is
delicious accompanied by a
mixed vegetable salad.

PASTRY
1¹/₂ cups/185 g/6 oz flour
1 cup/155 g/5 oz wholemeal flour
155 g/5 oz butter
1 egg, lightly beaten
2-3 tablespoons iced water

POTATO FILLING
2 onions, sliced
10 potatoes, thinly sliced
2 leeks, thinly sliced
500 g/1 lb sweet potatoes, thinly sliced
1 egg, lightly beaten
¹/₃ cup/90 g/3 oz sour cream
60 g/2 oz grated tasty cheese
(mature Cheddar)
2 tablespoons snipped fresh chives
milk
2 tablespoons sesame seeds

1 To make pastry, place flour, wholemeal flour and butter in a food processor and process until mixture resembles fine breadcrumbs. With machine running, add egg and enough water to form a soft dough. Turn dough onto a lightly floured surface and knead briefly. Wrap dough in plastic food wrap and refrigerate for 30 minutes.

2 Roll out two-thirds of pastry to fit a greased 18 cm/7 in springform tin.

3 For filling, arrange half the onions over base of pastry case, top with half the potatoes, leeks and sweet potatoes. Repeat layers. Place egg, sour cream, cheese and chives in a bowl, mix to combine and carefully pour over vegetables.

4 Roll out remaining pastry to make a lid for the pie. Place over filling, trim edges and pinch together to seal. Brush top of pie with a little milk and sprinkle with sesame seeds. Bake for 1 hour or until filling is cooked and pastry is golden. Serve hot, warm or cold.

Serves 6

Left: Two Potato Pie
Right: Chicken and Leek Roll

40

CHICKEN AND LEEK ROLL
Chicken

30 g/1 oz butter
3 leeks, sliced
125 g/4 oz button mushrooms, sliced
2 boneless chicken breast fillets, sliced
^{1}/3 cup/90 g/3 oz sour cream
1 tablespoon snipped fresh chives
freshly ground black pepper
12 sheets filo pastry
2 tablespoons olive oil
1 tablespoon poppy seeds

1   Melt butter in a frying pan over a medium heat, add leeks and cook, stirring, for 4 minutes or until leeks are golden. Add mushrooms and cook for 2 minutes longer or until mushrooms are soft. Remove from pan and set aside to cool.

2   Add chicken to pan and cook, stirring, for 5 minutes or until chicken is just cooked. Remove chicken from pan and set aside to cool.

3   Place leek mixture, chicken, sour cream, chives and black pepper to taste in a bowl and mix to combine.

4   Brush each pastry sheet with oil and layer. Spread filling over pastry leaving a 2 cm/^{3}/4 in border. Fold in sides and roll up like a Swiss roll. Place roll on a baking tray, brush with oil and sprinkle with poppy seeds. Bake for 20 minutes or until pastry is crisp and golden.

Serves 4

Oven temperature
200°C, 400°F, Gas 6

When fresh leeks are not available, a combination of spring onions and garlic can be used. Natural low-fat yogurt can be substituted for the sour cream, to make a lower-fat version of this recipe.

PASTA TO PLEASE

*Everybody loves pasta!
Whether you're looking
for hearty winter
warmers or light
and fresh sauces,
you'll find them here.
Quick and easy
to prepare, pasta
is perfect
for impromptu eating
and a great partner
to fish and chicken.*

MINESTRONE SALAD
Vegetarian

This dish makes the most of all the flavours ordinarily found in minestrone soup and serves them up as a salad! If plum (egg or Italian) tomatoes are not available, substitute ordinary tomatoes.

Dried chickpeas can be used in place of canned if you wish. To cook dried chickpeas see hint on page 35.

250 g/8 oz pasta shells
440 g/14 oz canned chickpeas, rinsed and drained
2 carrots, diced
2 zucchini (courgettes), diced
2 stalks celery, diced
1 red pepper, diced
155 g/5 oz green beans, blanched
3 plum (egg or Italian) tomatoes, cut into wedges
250 g/8 oz mixed lettuce leaves

PESTO DRESSING
125 g/4 oz ready-made pesto
$^{1}/_{2}$ cup/100 g/3$^{1}/_{2}$ oz natural yogurt
2 tablespoons mayonnaise

1 Cook pasta in boiling water in a large saucepan following packet directions. Drain, rinse under cold running water and set aside to cool completely.

2 Place chickpeas, carrots, zucchini (courgettes), celery, red pepper, beans, tomatoes and pasta in a bowl and toss to combine.

3 Arrange lettuce on a serving platter and top with pasta mixture.

4 To make dressing, place pesto, yogurt and mayonnaise in a bowl and mix to combine. Drizzle over salad and serve.

Serves 4

RAVIOLI WITH SUN-DRIED TOMATOES
Vegetarian

500 g/1 lb prepared spinach and ricotta ravioli
1 tablespoon olive oil
4 baby leeks, halved
1 tablespoon sun-dried tomato paste (pâté)
2 cups/500 mL/16 fl oz cream (double)
90 g/3 oz sun-dried tomatoes, sliced
125 g/4 oz grated Parmesan cheese
1 tablespoon chopped fresh basil
45 g/1$^{1}/_{2}$ oz pine nuts, toasted

Rich and flavoursome, sun-dried tomato paste (pâté) can be found in gourmet food and specialty shops and some supermarkets. If unavailable substitute ordinary tomato paste (purée).

1 Cook ravioli in boiling water in a large saucepan following packet directions. Drain and set aside to keep warm.

2 Heat oil in a frying pan over a medium heat, add leeks and cook, stirring, for 6 minutes or until leeks are golden. Stir sun-dried tomato paste (pâté), cream, sun-dried tomatoes and half the Parmesan cheese into pan. Bring to the boil, then reduce heat and simmer for 12 minutes or until sauce thickens slightly. To serve, spoon sauce over ravioli and sprinkle with basil, pine nuts and remaining Parmesan cheese.

Serves 4

Previous page: Minestrone Salad, Ravioli with Sun-dried Tomatoes
Right: Oriental Vegetable Noodles

ORIENTAL VEGETABLE NOODLES
Fish

315 g/10 oz fresh egg noodles
1 tablespoon sesame oil
1 clove garlic, crushed
1 tablespoon grated fresh ginger
185 g/6 oz firm white fish fillets, cut
into 2 cm/³/4 in pieces
155 g/5 oz green prawns, shelled and
deveined
4 spring onions, sliced
1 red pepper, sliced
250 g/8 oz bok choy (Chinese cabbage),
chopped
375 g/12 oz canned whole baby sweet
corn, drained
125 g/4 oz snow peas (mangetout)
125 g/4 oz fresh shiitake mushrooms,
sliced
2 tablespoons chopped fresh mint
2 tablespoons sweet chilli sauce
2 tablespoons sweet soy sauce
1 tablespoon plum sauce
1 tablespoon lime juice

1   Cook noodles in boiling water in a large saucepan following packet directions. Drain and set aside to keep warm.

2   Heat oil in a wok or large frying pan over a high heat, add garlic, ginger, fish and prawns and stir-fry for 2 minutes or until prawns just change colour.

3   Add spring onions, red pepper and bok choy (Chinese cabbage) to pan and stir-fry for 3 minutes longer. Add sweet corn, snow peas (mangetout), and mushrooms and stir-fry for 3 minutes.

4   Add mint, chilli sauce, soy sauce, plum sauce, lime juice and noodles and stir-fry for 3 minutes or until heated through. Serve immediately.

Serves 4

Sweet soy sauce, also known as kechap manis, is a thick sweet seasoning sauce used in Indonesian cooking. It is made of soy sauce, sugar and spices. If unavailable soy sauce or a mixture of soy sauce and dark corn syrup or golden syrup can be used in its place.

Plate Accoutrement

NOODLE FRITTATA
Fish

125 g/4 oz quick-cooking noodles
1 tablespoon sesame oil
1 tablespoon grated fresh ginger
3 spring onions, sliced
125 g/4 oz tofu, chopped
125 g/4 oz button mushrooms, sliced
220 g/7 oz fresh or canned crab meat,
flesh flaked
3 tablespoons chopped fresh coriander
1 tablespoon sweet chilli sauce
8 eggs, lightly beaten
$^1/_2$ cup/100 g/3$^1/_2$ oz natural yogurt
60 g/2 oz grated tasty cheese
(mature Cheddar)

1 Prepare noodles following packet directions. Drain and set aside.

2 Heat oil in a frying pan over a medium heat, add ginger and spring onions and cook, stirring, for 2 minutes. Add tofu and mushrooms and cook for 5 minutes or until tofu is golden. Add noodles, crab meat, coriander and chilli sauce and mix to combine.

3 Place eggs, yogurt and cheese in a bowl and mix to combine. Pour over mixture in frying pan and cook over a low heat for 8 minutes or until frittata is just set.

4 Place pan under a preheated hot grill and cook for 3 minutes or until top is golden. Serve immediately.

Serves 6

Quick-cooking noodles (or instant noodles) are available in packets in the Oriental food section of supermarkets. There are many varieties sold both with and without a flavouring sachet. In this recipe the noodles are prepared without the flavouring.

SPINACH FETTUCCINE LOAF
Vegetarian

Oven temperature
180°C, 350°F, Gas 4

250 g/8 oz fettuccine
3 eggs, lightly beaten
pinch cayenne pepper
1 cup/250 g/8 oz sour cream
6 tablespoons chopped fresh mixed herbs
1 bunch/500 g/1 lb English spinach,
leaves blanched and chopped
125 g/4 oz grated Gruyère cheese
90 g/3 oz pine nuts, toasted

1 Cook pasta in boiling water in a large saucepan following packet directions. Drain and set aside.

2 Place eggs, cayenne pepper, sour cream, herbs, spinach, Gruyère cheese and pine nuts in a bowl and mix to combine. Mix in pasta.

3 Spoon mixture into a greased 11 x 21 cm/4$^1/_2$ x 8$^1/_2$ in loaf tin and bake for 40 minutes or until firm. Stand in tin for 5 minutes before turning out and serving.

Serves 4

Look for a creamy-white colour, when purchasing pine nuts, as a grey colour indicates rancidity. Store pine nuts, like all seeds, in a tightly closed container in the refrigerator to maintain freshness and flavour.

Plates Limoges Australia

Noodle Frittata, Spinach Fettuccine Loaf

CHICKEN PASTA GRATIN

Chicken

Oven temperature
180°C, 350°F, Gas 4

This easy family dish can be prepared several hours in advance. Cover dish with its lid or heavy-duty foil and refrigerate. To reheat, bake, covered at 180°C/350°F/Gas 4 for 30 minutes, then uncover and bake for 20-30 minutes longer or until bubbly and brown.

6 plum (egg or Italian) tomatoes, halved
1 tablespoon vegetable oil
315 g/10 oz wholemeal pasta shapes
30 g/1 oz butter
1 clove garlic, crushed
1 red onion, sliced
2 boneless chicken breast fillets, sliced
$^{1}/_{4}$ cup/60 mL/2 fl oz white wine
$1^{1}/_{4}$ cups/315 mL/10 fl oz cream (double)
1 tablespoon chopped fresh tarragon or 1 teaspoon dried tarragon
125 g/4 oz grated tasty cheese (mature Cheddar)
freshly ground black pepper
30 g/1 oz grated Parmesan cheese

1 Brush tomatoes with oil and cook under a preheated hot grill for 10 minutes or until soft and browned. Set aside.

2 Cook pasta in boiling water in a large saucepan following packet directions, drain and set aside.

3 Melt butter in a frying pan over a medium heat, add garlic and onion and cook, stirring, for 3 minutes or until onion is soft and golden. Add chicken and cook, stirring, for 6 minutes longer or until chicken is tender.

4 Stir wine, cream and tarragon into pan and bring to the boil. Reduce heat and simmer for 10 minutes. Remove pan from heat, add tomatoes, pasta, half the tasty cheese (mature Cheddar) and black pepper to taste and mix gently to combine.

5 Spoon mixture into a greased 8 cup/ 2 litre/$3^{1}/_{2}$ pt capacity ovenproof dish. Combine remaining tasty cheese (mature Cheddar) and Parmesan cheese and sprinkle over pasta mixture. Bake for 20 minutes or until cheese melts and is golden.

Serves 4

Plate Limoges Australia

Left: Chicken Pasta Gratin
Right: Pasta with Roasted Shallots

PASTA WITH ROASTED SHALLOTS
Fish

12 shallots or pickling onions, peeled
6 cloves garlic, peeled
6 spring onions, halved lengthwise
1 tablespoon olive oil
1 tablespoon hazelnut or vegetable oil
250 g/8 oz firm white fish fillets, cut
into 3 cm/1¹/₂ in pieces
250 g/8 oz broccoli florets
250 g/8 oz asparagus spears, halved
2 zucchini (courgettes), sliced
155 g/5 oz sugar snap peas
500 g/1 lb tagliatelle

1   Place shallots or pickling onions, garlic and spring onions in a baking dish, sprinkle with olive oil and bake for 30 minutes or until golden.

2   Heat hazelnut or vegetable oil in a frying pan over a medium heat, add fish and cook, turning several times, for 4 minutes or until fish is cooked. Remove fish from pan and set aside. Add broccoli, asparagus, zucchini (courgettes) and sugar snap peas to pan and cook, stirring, for 5 minutes or until vegetables just tender.

3   Cook tagliatelle in boiling water in a large saucepan following packet directions. Drain. Divide tagliatelle between serving plates, then top with baked vegetables and green vegetable mixture.

Serves 6

Oven temperature
180°C, 350°F, Gas 4

This assortment of 'greens' can easily be replaced with 'yellows' – such as a combination of carrots, yellow peppers, squash and pumpkin, if you prefer.

Above: Leek and Mushroom Soup
Right: Ricotta Herb Fettuccine

LEEK AND MUSHROOM SOUP
Vegetarian

45 g/1^1/2 oz butter
2 leeks, thinly sliced
1 tablespoon yellow mustard seeds
250 g/8 oz button mushrooms, sliced
2 tablespoons chopped fresh thyme or
2 teaspoons dried thyme
4 cups/1 litre/1^3/4 pt vegetable stock
125 g/4 oz risoni pasta
^{1}/2 cup/125 mL/4 fl oz cream (double)

Risoni pasta is a small rice shaped pasta used mainly in soups. Any other small shaped pasta can be used instead.

1   Melt butter in a large saucepan over a medium heat, add leeks and mustard seeds and cook, stirring, for 5 minutes or until leeks are soft and golden.

2   Add mushrooms and thyme to pan and cook for 5 minutes longer. Add stock and pasta, bring to the boil, then reduce heat and simmer for 15 minutes or until pasta is tender. Stir in cream and simmer for 5 minutes longer.

Serves 4

RICOTTA HERB FETTUCCINE

Vegetarian

350 g/11 oz fettuccine
155 g/5 oz ricotta cheese
60 g/2 oz grated Pecorino cheese
30 g/1 oz butter
1 tablespoon finely grated orange rind
2 tablespoons snipped fresh chives
2 tablespoons chopped fresh thyme or
2 teaspoons dried thyme
2 tablespoons chopped fresh parsley
freshly ground black pepper

1   Cook pasta in boiling water in a large saucepan following packet directions. Drain and place in a bowl.

2   Combine ricotta cheese, Pecorino cheese, butter, orange rind, chives, thyme, parsley and black pepper to taste. Add ricotta mixture to pasta and toss to combine.

3   Spoon mixture into an 8 cup/2 litre/ $3^1/2$ pt capacity ovenproof dish, cover with aluminium foil and bake for 8-10 minutes or until mixture is heated through.

Serves 4

Oven temperature
180°C, 350°F, Gas 4

For a complete meal, serve this fettuccine dish with wholegrain bread or rolls and a tossed green salad.

Plate Limoges Australia

CURRY
FEAST

*Lentil Fritters
with Chilli Yogurt*

*Spiced
Spinach Pastries*

*Bean and Tofu
Curry*

*Chicken and Potato
Curry*

Spiced Lentils

Steamed Rice

Lemon Yogurt Cake

Serves 6

LENTIL FRITTERS WITH CHILLI YOGURT
Vegetarian

Previous page: Bean and Tofu Curry, Chicken and Potato Curry with Spiced Lentils, Lentil Fritters, Spiced Spinach Pastries

125 g/4 oz red lentils, cooked
4 spring onions, chopped
1 carrot, grated
2 zucchini (courgettes), grated
$^1/_2$ cup/60 g/2 oz besan flour
2 tablespoons chopped fresh coriander
1 teaspoon cumin seeds
2 eggs, lightly beaten
$^1/_4$ cup/60 mL/2 fl oz milk
vegetable oil, for shallow frying

CHILLI YOGURT
1 cup/200 g/6$^1/_2$ oz natural yogurt
1 fresh green chilli, finely chopped
1 fresh red chilli, finely chopped
1 teaspoon ground cumin

1 Place lentils, spring onions, carrot, zucchini (courgettes), flour, coriander and cumin seeds in a bowl and mix to combine. Add eggs and milk and mix well.

2 Heat 5 cm/2 in oil in a frying pan until a cube of bread dropped in browns in 50 seconds. Add tablespoons of lentil mixture and cook for 3 minutes each side or until golden. Drain on absorbent kitchen paper. Repeat to use remaining mixture.

3 To make Chilli Yogurt, combine yogurt, red and green chillies and cumin in a bowl. Serve with fritters.

Makes 20

To allow the flavour time to develop, make the Chilli Yoghurt in advance, cover with plastic food wrap and refrigerate. Serve chilled. Besan flour is made from chickpeas and is available from Indian and Oriental food stores.

SPICED SPINACH PASTRIES
Vegetarian

375 g/12 oz prepared puff pastry
mango chutney

SPINACH FILLING
2 teaspoons vegetable oil
1 onion, chopped
1 tablespoon black mustard seeds
2 teaspoons curry paste
10 large spinach leaves, chopped
125 g/4 oz cottage cheese
60 g/2 oz frozen peas

1 To make filling, heat oil in a frying pan over a medium heat, add onion, mustard seeds and curry paste and cook, stirring, for 3 minutes or until onion is soft.

2 Add spinach to pan and cook for 8 minutes longer or until liquid from spinach evaporates. Stir in cottage cheese and peas. Remove pan from heat and set aside to cool.

3 Roll out pastry to 3 mm/$^1/_8$ in thick and using a 10 cm/4 in cutter, cut out rounds. Place a spoonful of filling in the centre of each pastry round. Brush edges lightly with water, fold pastry over filling and press edges together to seal. Place pastries on greased baking trays and bake for 12 minutes or until pastry is puffed and golden. Serve warm with mango chutney.

Oven temperature
180°C, 350°F, Gas 4

Substitute any leftover cooked peas for the frozen quantity in this recipe. If silverbeet (spinach) is unavailable, frozen spinach, thawed and drained on absorbent kitchen paper, may be used instead.

Makes 25

Lentil Fritters with Chilli Yogurt

BEAN AND TOFU CURRY
Vegetarian

1 tablespoon peanut oil
2 onions, sliced
1 tablespoon finely grated fresh ginger
1 tablespoon mild curry paste
1 teaspoon ground cinnamon
2 x 440 g/14 oz canned peeled tomatoes,
undrained and mashed
$^3/_4$ cup/185 mL/6 fl oz vegetable stock
440 g/14 oz canned red kidney beans,
rinsed and drained
440 g/14 oz canned chickpeas, rinsed
and drained
440 g/14 oz canned butter beans, rinsed
and drained
315 g/10 oz tofu, fried and chopped
90 g/3 oz chopped roasted peanuts
185 g/6 oz green beans, halved

1   Heat oil in a saucepan over a medium heat, add onions, ginger, curry paste and cinnamon and cook, stirring, for 3 minutes or until onion is soft.

2   Add tomatoes and stock to pan, bring to the boil, then reduce heat and simmer for 5 minutes. Add red kidney beans, chickpeas and butter beans and simmer for 8 minutes longer.

3   Stir in tofu, peanuts and green beans, reduce heat to low and simmer gently for 5 minutes or until heated through.

Serves 6

For information on frying tofu see hint on page 18.

CHICKEN AND POTATO CURRY
Chicken

2 teaspoons vegetable oil
2 cloves garlic, crushed
2 fresh red chillies, chopped
1 teaspoon ground cumin
1 teaspoon ground coriander
$^1/_2$ teaspoon turmeric
$^1/_2$ teaspoon ground cardamom
3 boneless chicken breast fillets, sliced
2 cups/500 mL/16 fl oz chicken stock
1$^1/_4$ cups/315 mL/10 fl oz coconut milk
6 potatoes, chopped
1 red pepper, chopped
2 teaspoons garam masala

1 Heat oil in a saucepan over a medium heat, add garlic, chillies, cumin, coriander, turmeric and cardamom and cook, stirring, for 2 minutes.

2 Add chicken to pan and cook, stirring, for 4 minutes or until chicken is brown. Add stock, coconut milk, potatoes and red pepper and mix to combine. Bring to the boil, then reduce heat and simmer for 20 minutes or until potatoes are tender and curry thickens. Stir in garam marsala.

Serves 6

This dish can be made the day before and reheated when required. Flat breads, such as naan, are available from Indian food shops and some supermarkets. All you need to do is heat them before serving.

SPICED LENTILS
Vegetarian

500 g/1 lb green lentils
2 teaspoons vegetable oil
2 fresh green chillies, chopped
2 cloves garlic, crushed
1 tablespoon grated fresh ginger
1 tablespoon yellow mustard seeds
1 tablespoon ground cumin
3 tablespoons chopped fresh coriander
$^1/_2$ cup/125 mL/4 fl oz vegetable stock
$^1/_2$ cup/100 g/3$^1/_2$ oz natural yogurt

1 Bring a large saucepan of water to the boil. Add lentils, reduce heat and simmer for 15 minutes or until lentils are tender. Drain and set aside.

2 Heat oil in a frying pan over a medium heat, add chillies, garlic, ginger, mustard seeds, cumin and coriander and cook, stirring, for 2 minutes.

3 Add lentils and stock to pan and cook for 5 minutes longer or until stock is absorbed. Serve with yogurt.

Serves 6

You may like to include slices of cucumber with the natural yogurt which accompanies this dish to cool the heat of the chilli.

LEMON YOGURT CAKE

Vegetarian

185 g/6 oz butter
³/4 cup/185 g/6 oz sugar
1 tablespoon finely grated lemon rind
1 teaspoon vanilla essence
2 eggs, lightly beaten
2¹/4 cups/280 g/9 oz self-raising flour, sifted
¹/4 cup/60 mL/2 fl oz lemon juice
1 cup/200 g/6¹/2 oz natural yogurt

LEMON SYRUP
1 cup/250 g/8 oz sugar
¹/2 cup/125 mL/4 fl oz lemon juice

Makes a 23 cm/9 in ring cake

1 Place butter, sugar, lemon rind and vanilla essence in a bowl and beat until light and creamy. Add eggs one at a time, beating well after each addition.

2 Add flour, lemon juice and yogurt and mix to combine. Pour batter into a greased 23 cm/9 in fluted ring tin and bake for 1 hour or until cake is cooked when tested with a skewer.

3 To make syrup, place sugar and lemon juice in a saucepan and cook over a low heat, stirring constantly, until sugar dissolves. Bring to the boil and cook, without stirring, for 4 minutes or until mixture thickens slightly. Pour hot syrup over hot cake in tin. Stand for 5 minutes before turning onto a serving plate.

Lemon Yogurt Cake

Oven temperature
190°C, 375°F, Gas 5

To test if your cake is cooked, insert a skewer into the thickest part of the cake. If the skewer comes away clean, your cake is cooked. If there is still cake mixture on the skewer, cook for 5 minutes longer then test again.

SUMMER BARBECUE

Vegetable Kebabs

Summer Corn Bread

*Bay
and Lime Fish*

*Barbecue
Herb Ricotta*

*Char-grilled
Vegetable Salad*

Summer Rice Salad

Rum Coconut Cake

Barbecue Bananas

Serves 6

VEGETABLE KEBABS
Vegetarian

4 zucchini (courgettes), cut into
thick slices
1 red pepper, cut into chunks
250 g/8 oz button mushrooms
250 g/8 oz cherry tomatoes
1 red onion, cut into wedges
4 nectarines, cut into wedges

SOY AND HONEY MARINADE
2 tablespoons soy sauce
2 tablespoons honey
1 tablespoon sesame oil

1 To make marinade place soy sauce, honey and oil in a bowl and mix to combine. Set aside.

2 Thread zucchini (courgettes), red pepper, mushrooms, tomatoes, onion and nectarines onto lightly oiled skewers.

3 Brush kebabs with marinade and cook on a preheated hot barbecue grill for 5 minutes or until cooked to your liking.

Serves 6

If nectarines are not available, substitute any firm fleshy stone fruit such as peaches, mangoes, pears or pineapple. Alternatively, you may wish to do without the fruit portion altogether!

SUMMER CORN BREAD
Vegetarian

60 g/2 oz butter, melted
2 tablespoons vegetable oil
4 spring onions, chopped
2 pieces canned red pepper or
1 red pepper, roasted and skin removed,
chopped
125 g/4 oz canned sweet corn kernels,
drained
60 g/2 oz pitted black olives, chopped
6 tablespoons chopped fresh basil
1 cup/250 mL/8 fl oz milk
1 egg, lightly beaten
1 cup/125 g/4 oz self-raising flour
1 cup/170 g/5^1/$_2$ oz corn meal (polenta)
2 teaspoons baking powder
125 g/4 oz grated tasty cheese
(mature Cheddar)

1 Place butter, oil, spring onions, red pepper, sweet corn, olives, basil, milk and egg in a bowl and mix to combine.

2 Sift together flour, corn meal (polenta) and baking powder. Add to vegetable mixture and mix well.

3 Pour mixture into a greased 23 cm/ 9 in square cake tin, sprinkle with cheese and bake for 35 minutes or until bread is cooked when tested with a skewer.

Makes a 23 cm/9 in square loaf

Oven temperature
200°C, 400°F, Gas 6

If you have a kettle barbecue you can cook this bread in it rather than in the oven.

*Previous page: Bay and Lime Fish, Char-grilled
Vegetable Salad, Summer Rice Salad
Right: Vegetable Kebabs, Summer Corn Bread*

BAY AND LIME FISH
Fish

6 small firm white fish fillets
sweet corn husks or aluminium foil
12 slices lime
12 fresh bay leaves
1 fresh red chilli, chopped
freshly ground black pepper

When buying fish fillets, look for those that are shiny and firm with a pleasant sea smell. Avoid fillets that are dull, soft, discoloured or 'ooze' water when touched.

1   Place fish fillets in sweet corn husks or, if using aluminium foil, cut six pieces large enough to completely enclose the fillets, then place a fillet on each piece. Top each fillet with 2 slices lime, 2 bay leaves and chilli and black pepper to taste. Tie ends of husks or fold foil to encase fish.

2   Cook parcels on a preheated hot barbecue for 8 minutes or until fish flakes when tested with a fork.

Serves 6

BARBECUE HERB RICOTTA
Vegetarian

750 g/1¹/₂ lb fresh ricotta cheese in
one piece
2 tablespoons olive oil
2 tablespoons paprika
2 tablespoons chopped fresh oregano or
marjoram
2 tablespoons chopped fresh parsley
freshly ground black pepper

This recipe is a great starter for outdoor barbecues or, when served with a crisp green salad, a novel light luncheon dish.
Fresh ricotta cheese is available from delicatessens. Take care when handling as it is quite fragile, however once baked it becomes firm.

1   Place ricotta cheese on a wire rack and set aside to drain for 1 hour. Place ricotta cheese on a baking tray and brush with olive oil. Combine paprika, oregano or marjoram, parsley and black pepper to taste and sprinkle over ricotta.

2   Cook ricotta cheese in preheated hot kettle barbecue and cook for 20 minutes or until cheese is golden. Alternatively, cover tray and cheese with aluminium foil and cook on the barbecue grill or bake in the oven at 180°C/350°F/Gas 4.

Serves 6

Barbecue Herb Ricotta

CHAR-GRILLED VEGETABLE SALAD

Vegetarian

2 cobs fresh sweet corn, cut into
3 cm/1¹/4 in pieces
6 baby eggplant (aubergines), halved
lengthwise
3 red peppers, cut into quarters
6 zucchini (courgettes), halved
lengthwise
6 small leeks, halved lengthwise
olive oil

HERB DRESSING
2 tablespoons chopped fresh basil
1 tablespoon chopped fresh rosemary or
1 teaspoon dried rosemary
2 tablespoons chilli oil
2 tablespoons balsamic vinegar

1   Brush sweet corn cobs, eggplant
(aubergines), red peppers, zucchini
(courgettes) and leeks with olive oil. Place
vegetables on a preheated hot barbecue
and cook, turning occasionally, for 15
minutes or until vegetables are golden and
tender.

2   To make dressing, place basil,
rosemary, chilli oil and vinegar in a
screwtop jar and shake well to combine.
Drizzle dressing over warm vegetables.

Serves 6

Smoky flavoured, crisp on the
outside and tender within,
char-grilled vegetables taste
quite unlike any other. You
may substitute the
proportions of vegetables
listed here if any of them are
in short supply.

Summer Rice Salad

Vegetarian

2 cups/440 g/14 oz long grain rice,
cooked and cooled
1 small pineapple, flesh chopped
440 g/14 oz canned chickpeas, rinsed
and drained
2 mangoes, peeled and sliced
4 spring onions, chopped
1 red pepper, sliced
2 tablespoons chopped fresh mint
60 g/2 oz flaked almonds, toasted
3 tablespoons reduced-salt soy sauce

Place rice, pineapple, chickpeas, mangoes, spring onions, red pepper, mint and almonds in a salad bowl. Sprinkle with soy sauce and toss to combine. Cover and refrigerate until ready to serve.

Serves 6

If canned chickpeas are unavailable, use cold cooked chickpeas instead. To cook dried chickpeas see hint on page 35.

Rum Coconut Cake

Vegetarian

Oven temperature
180°C, 350°F, Gas 4

1^1/2 cups/185 g/6 oz self-raising flour
^{1}/2 teaspoon baking powder
60 g/2 oz shredded coconut
1 cup/220 g/7 oz caster sugar
2 eggs, lightly beaten
1 cup/200 g/6^1/2 oz natural yogurt
1 cup/250 mL/8 fl oz milk

RUM SYRUP
1 cup/220 g/7 oz caster sugar
^{3}/4 cup/185 mL/6 fl oz water
^{1}/4 cup/60 mL/2 fl oz coconut-flavoured
rum

1 Sift flour and baking powder together into a bowl. Add coconut and sugar and mix to combine.

2 Place eggs, yogurt and milk in a bowl and whisk to combine. Add to dry ingredients and mix until smooth.

3 Spoon batter into a greased and lined 23 cm/9 in round cake tin and bake for 1 hour or until cooked when tested with a skewer.

4 To make syrup, place sugar, water and rum in a saucepan and cook over a low heat, stirring constantly, for 4-5 minutes or until sugar dissolves. Bring to the boil, then reduce heat and simmer for 4 minutes or until syrup thickens slightly. Pour half the hot syrup over hot cake in tin. Stand cake in tin for 5 minutes before turning onto a serving platter. Serve with remaining syrup.

Makes a 23 cm/9 in round cake

If coconut-flavoured rum is unavailable, orange-flavoured liqueur is a suitable substitute.

Plates Limoges Australia

Rum Coconut Cake,
Barbecue Bananas

BARBECUE BANANAS
Vegetarian

6 bananas, halved lengthwise
60 g/2 oz butter, melted
¹/₄ cup/45 g/1¹/₂ oz brown sugar
¹/₄ cup/60 mL/2 fl oz dark rum
1 tablespoon lime juice

Place bananas, butter, sugar, rum and lime juice in a baking tin. Cook on a preheated hot barbecue, turning bananas several times, for 5 minutes or until bananas and syrup are golden.

Serves 6

For a rich treat, serve Barbecue Bananas with whipped cream. Alternatively, a spoonful of natural yogurt lends a refreshing sharp contrast to their sweet rum flavour.

65

MIDDLE EASTERN BANQUET

Baba Ganoush

Red Pepper Hummus

Selection of breads
such as pitta, Lebanese,
Turkish flat bread

Feta Cheese Pastries

Felafel

Middle Eastern Peppers

Chicken Moussaka

Tabbouleh

Pistachio Cheesecake

Serves 8

BABA GANOUSH
Vegetarian

Oven temperature
200°C, 400°F, Gas 6

Do not pierce the eggplant (aubergines) before baking. The intense heat should ideally char the outside of the eggplant (aubergines) and so lend a delicious smoky flavour to the flesh inside.

2 eggplant (aubergines)
$^1/_2$ cup/125 g/4 oz tahini paste
$^1/_2$ cup/100 g/3$^1/_2$ oz natural yogurt
$^1/_3$ cup/90 mL/3 fl oz lemon juice
2 cloves garlic, crushed
2 tablespoons chopped fresh parsley

1   Place eggplant (aubergines) on a baking tray and bake for 30 minutes or until tender. Set aside to cool. Cut eggplant (aubergines) in half and scoop out flesh.

2   Place eggplant (aubergine) flesh, tahini paste, yogurt, lemon juice and garlic in a food processor or blender and process until smooth. Transfer mixture to a serving bowl and sprinkle with parsley.

Serves 8

RED PEPPER HUMMUS
Vegetarian

625 g/1$^1/_4$ lb dried chickpeas
4 cloves garlic, crushed
60 g/2 oz sun-dried peppers, chopped
$^1/_2$ cup/125 mL/4 fl oz lemon juice
$^1/_2$ cup/125 mL/4 fl oz olive oil

1   Place chickpeas in a large bowl, cover with cold water and set aside to soak overnight. Drain and place chickpeas in large saucepan, cover with water and bring to the boil. Boil for 10 minutes, then reduce heat and simmer for 45-60 minutes or until chickpeas are tender. Drain and set aside to cool.

2   Place chickpeas, garlic, sun-dried peppers, lemon juice and oil in a food processor and process until smooth.

Serves 8

Sun-dried peppers are available from gourmet food and specialty shops. If unavailable, substitute roasted peppers (see hint on page 23 for roasting peppers) or use sun-dried tomatoes instead.

Previous page: Chicken Moussaka, Felafel, Middle Eastern Peppers, Baba Ganoush, Red Pepper Hummus
Orange plate with green rim and plain green plate Limoges Australia

FETA CHEESE PASTRIES

Vegetarian

375 g/12 oz filo pastry
vegetable oil

FETA AND CORIANDER FILLING
200 g/6¹/₂ oz feta cheese, crumbled
1 egg, lightly beaten
2 tablespoons sultanas
1 tablespoon chopped fresh coriander
1 teaspoon ground nutmeg

1 To make filling, place feta cheese, egg, sultanas, coriander and nutmeg in a bowl and mix to combine.

2 Layer 6 sheets of pastry, brushing each with oil. Cut pastry into four strips lengthwise. Place a tablespoon of filling on one end of each pastry strip and roll up tucking in sides to make a thin roll. Repeat with remaining pastry and filling to use all ingredients.

3 Place pastries on a greased baking tray, brush with oil and bake for 15 minutes or until pastry is crisp and golden.

Oven temperature
190°C, 375°F, Gas 5

There are many different varieties of feta available and depending on the way they are made, some are more salty and others, more creamy in flavour. For many people, the piquancy of feta is one of its most popular characteristics. Get to know the different tastes by asking if you may sample a small piece before buying.

Feta Cheese Pastries

Makes 32

Plate Limoges Australia

69

FELAFEL

Vegetarian

440 g/14 oz chickpeas
3 cloves garlic, crushed
1 small onion, chopped
4 spring onions, chopped
2 tablespoons chopped fresh coriander
2 tablespoons chopped fresh parsley
1 teaspoon ground cumin
$^1/_2$ teaspoon turmeric
vegetable oil, for deep frying

1 Place chickpeas in a large bowl, cover with cold water and set aside to soak overnight. Drain. Place chickpeas in large saucepan, cover with water and bring to the boil. Boil for 10 minutes, then reduce heat and simmer for 45-60 minutes or until chickpeas are tender. Drain and set aside to cool.

2 Place chickpeas, garlic, onion, spring onions, coriander, parsley, cumin and turmeric in a food processor or blender and process to combine.

3 Heat oil in a large saucepan until a cube of bread dropped in browns in 50 seconds. Shape tablespoons of chickpea mixture into balls and deep-fry, a few at a time, for 3 minutes or until golden brown. Drain on absorbent kitchen paper.

Serves 8

To speed preparation, omit Step 1 and use canned chickpeas. You will need two 440 g/14 oz cans and the chickpeas should be drained and rinsed before making the felafel.

MIDDLE EASTERN PEPPERS

Vegetarian

olive oil
3 onions, sliced
1 teaspoon sugar
1 cup/220 g/7 oz rice, cooked
2 tomatoes, chopped
2 tablespoons pine nuts, toasted
2 tablespoons chopped fresh dill or
2 teaspoons dried dill
2 tablespoons currants
1 tablespoon chopped fresh mint
8 mixed red, green and yellow peppers

1 Heat 2 tablespoons oil in a frying pan over a medium heat, add onions and sugar and cook, stirring, for 8 minutes or until sugar dissolves and onions are soft and caramelised.

2 Add rice, tomatoes, pine nuts, dill, currants and mint to pan and cook for 5 minutes.

3 Cut red, green and yellow peppers in half lengthwise and remove seeds and membranes. Brush peppers with a little oil and place on a greased baking tray. Divide rice mixture between pepper shells and bake for 30 minutes or until peppers are tender.

Serves 8

Oven temperature
180°C, 350°F, Gas 4

Toasting pine nuts gives them a delicious flavour. The quickest method is to spread them in a thin layer on a baking tray, place under a preheated hot grill and toast until golden. Turn them several times during cooking to ensure all sides are toasted and to prevent burning. Set aside to cool.

CHICKEN MOUSSAKA
Chicken

4 large eggplant (aubergines),
thinly sliced
salt
3 tablespoons olive oil
2 cloves garlic, crushed
1 onion, chopped
500 g/1 lb chicken mince
2 x 440 g/14 oz canned peeled tomatoes,
undrained and mashed
500 g/1 lb potatoes, thinly sliced
$^{1}/_{2}$ cup/30 g/1 oz breadcrumbs, made
from stale bread
60 g/2 oz grated Parmesan cheese

CHEESE SAUCE
30 g/1 oz butter
2 tablespoons flour
$1^{1}/_{4}$ cups/315 mL/10 fl oz milk
60 g/2 oz grated tasty cheese
(mature Cheddar)

1   Place eggplant (aubergine) slices in a colander set over a bowl and sprinkle with salt. Set aside to stand for 10 minutes then rinse under cold running water and pat dry with absorbent kitchen paper.

2   Heat 2 tablespoons oil in a frying pan over a medium heat and cook eggplant (aubergine) slices in batches for 2 minutes each side or until golden. Set aside.

3   Heat remaining oil in frying pan, add garlic and onion and cook, stirring, for 3 minutes or until onion is soft and golden. Add chicken and cook, stirring, for 5 minutes or until chicken browns. Stir in tomatoes and bring to the boil. Reduce heat and simmer for 15 minutes, or until mixture reduces and thickens. Remove pan from heat and set aside to cool.

4   To make sauce, melt butter in a saucepan over a medium heat, stir in flour and cook for 1 minute. Remove pan from heat and gradually stir in milk. Return pan to heat and cook, stirring constantly, until sauce boils and thickens. Remove pan from heat and stir in tasty cheese (mature Cheddar).

5   Arrange half the eggplant (aubergine) slices over base of a 10 cup/$2^{1}/_{2}$ litre/4 pt capacity ovenproof dish. Top with half the chicken mixture, half the potatoes and half the cheese sauce. Repeat layers to use all ingredients. Combine breadcrumbs and Parmesan cheese and sprinkle over moussaka. Bake for 50 minutes or until top is golden and moussaka is cooked through.

Serves 8

Oven temperature
180°C, 350°F, Gas 4

The addition of chicken to this moussaka recipe is a refreshing alternative to a traditional dish which is more often made with lamb or beef mince.

Red Pepper Hummus, Chicken Moussaka

TABBOULEH
Vegetarian

185 g/6 oz burghul (cracked wheat)
2 cups/500 mL/16 fl oz water
1/2 bunch fresh flat-leaf parsley, chopped
1/2 bunch fresh mint, leaves chopped
6 spring onions, chopped
3 tomatoes, chopped
1/4 cup/60 mL/2 fl oz lemon juice
2 tablespoons olive oil
freshly ground black pepper

1   Place burghul (cracked wheat) and water in a bowl and set aside for 8-10 minutes or until water is absorbed.

2   Place burghul (cracked wheat), parsley, mint, spring onions and tomatoes in a bowl. Combine lemon juice, olive oil and black pepper to taste, pour over burghul (cracked wheat) mixture and toss to combine. Cover and refrigerate until ready to serve.

Serves 8

This salad relies quite heavily on the flavour of fresh herbs, so dried herbs are not an appropriate substitute. If fresh mint is unavailable, try substituting chopped fresh coriander instead.

PISTACHIO CHEESECAKE
Vegetarian

90 g/3 oz chopped walnuts
185 g/6 oz chopped pistachio nuts
1 cup/170 g/5 1/2 oz brown sugar
375 g/12 oz filo pastry
125 g/4 oz butter, melted
250 g/8 oz ricotta cheese
1 teaspoon rosewater

SUGAR SYRUP
2 cups/440 g/14 oz caster sugar
1 cup/250 mL/8 fl oz water

1   Place walnuts, 90 g/3 oz pistachio nuts and brown sugar in a bowl and mix to combine. Set aside.

2   Cut ten 20 cm/8 in circles from filo pastry. Place one circle of pastry in a greased and lined 20 cm/8 in round sandwich tin, brush with butter and sprinkle with nut mixture. Repeat layers to use half the pastry and half the nut mixture. In a second greased and lined 20 cm/8 in round sandwich tin layer the remaining pastry and nut mixture in the same way. Bake pastry stacks for 30 minutes or until pastry is golden.

3   To make syrup, place caster sugar and water in a saucepan and heat, stirring constantly, over a medium heat until sugar dissolves. Bring mixture to simmering and simmer for 10 minutes or until syrup thickens. Pour hot syrup over hot pastry in tin. Cool in tin.

4   Place ricotta cheese and rosewater in a bowl and beat to combine. Spread half the mixture over one pastry stack. Top with other pastry stack, spread with remaining ricotta mixture and sprinkle with remaining pistachio nuts.

Serves 8

Oven temperature
180°C, 350°F, Gas 4

Rosewater is an essential ingredient in Middle Eastern and Indian cooking and is used in both savoury and sweet dishes. It become fashionable as a flavouring in England during the 16th century and remained a staple ingredient until Victorian times. Rosewater is available from Middle Eastern and Indian food shops and some pharmacies.

Pistachio Cheesecake

SPECIAL DINNER

*Salad
of Roast Tomatoes*

Olive Bruschetta

Cajun Spiced Fish

Semolina Cheese Bake

Caramelised Leeks

*Fruit
with Passion Fruit
Custard*

Serves 4

SALAD OF ROAST TOMATOES

Vegetarian

Oven temperature
180°C, 350°F, Gas 4

6 plum (egg or Italian) tomatoes, halved
8 cloves garlic, peeled
freshly ground black pepper
2 tablespoons olive oil
315 g/10 oz assorted lettuce leaves
185 g/6 oz feta cheese, crumbled
1 yellow or red pepper, sliced

TANGY DRESSING
3 tablespoons balsamic or red wine vinegar
3 tablespoons tomato purée
3 drops Tabasco sauce

1 Place tomatoes and garlic on a baking tray, sprinkle with black pepper to taste and oil and bake for 30 minutes or until tomatoes are soft and golden. Set aside to cool completely.

2 Arrange lettuce leaves, feta cheese, yellow or red pepper, tomatoes and garlic attractively on serving plates.

3 To make dressing, place vinegar, tomato purée, Tabasco and black pepper to taste in a screwtop jar and shake well to combine. Drizzle dressing over salad and serve immediately.

Serves 4

The sweet rich flavour of roast tomatoes is a perfect partner for the creamy piquant feta cheese in this salad.

OLIVE BRUSCHETTA

Vegetarian

8 slices crusty Italian bread
olive oil
3 spring onions, chopped
75 g/2½ oz black olives, pitted and chopped
3 tablespoons chopped fresh parsley
1 tablespoon lemon juice
freshly ground black pepper

1 Brush bread with oil and cook under a preheated hot grill until golden on both sides. Set aside to keep warm.

2 Heat 2 teaspoons oil in a frying pan over a medium heat, add spring onions and cook, stirring, for 2 minutes. Add olives, parsley, lemon juice and black pepper to taste and cook, stirring, for 4 minutes or until heated through. Top toast with olive mixture and serve immediately.

Serves 4

Bruschetta is fast overtaking garlic bread as the favourite bread accompaniment. This recipe is an ideal way to make use of any leftover crusty bread loaf, if Italian is not available.

*Previous page: Caramelised Leeks,
Cajun Spiced Fish, Semolina Cheese Bake
Right: Olive Bruschetta, Salad of Roast Tomatoes*

CAJUN SPICED FISH

Fish

4 small firm white fish fillets
1 tablespoon vegetable oil

CAJUN SPICE
2 teaspoons paprika
2 teaspoons freshly ground black pepper
1 teaspoon ground coriander
1 teaspoon ground cumin
$^1/_2$ teaspoon chilli powder

1   To make Cajun Spice, place paprika, black pepper, coriander, cumin, and chilli powder in a bowl and mix to combine.

2   Toss fish in spice mixture to coat. Heat oil in a frying pan over a medium heat, add fish and cook for 2 minutes each side or until flesh flakes when tested with a fork.

Serves 4

Serve this dish garnished with wedges of lime or lemon.

Semolina Cheese Bake

Vegetarian

Oven temperature
190°C, 375°F, Gas 5

1 1/2 cups/375 mL/12 fl oz milk
3/4 cup/125 g/4 oz semolina
60 g/2 oz grated tasty cheese
(mature Cheddar)
1 egg, lightly beaten
freshly ground black pepper
3/4 cup/185 g/6 oz sour cream
125 g/4 oz grated smoked cheese

1 Place milk in a saucepan and heat over a medium heat until almost boiling. Gradually stir in semolina and continue to cook, stirring constantly, until mixture is very thick.

2 Remove pan from heat and stir in tasty cheese (mature Cheddar), egg and black pepper to taste. Spread mixture over the base of a greased 20 cm/8 in square cake tin and refrigerate until firm.

3 Turn semolina mixture out of tin and cut into triangles. Place triangles on a baking tray, spread each with sour cream and sprinkle with smoked cheese. Bake for 20 minutes or until cheese melts and is golden.

Serves 4

To remove the semolina from the tin more easily, line the greased tin with aluminium foil, leaving the foil overhanging a little on two opposite sides to make handles for lifting.

Caramelised Leeks

Vegetarian

1 tablespoon vegetable oil
4 baby leeks, sliced lengthwise
2 tablespoons brown sugar
1/2 cup/125 mL/4 fl oz dry white wine
1 tablespoon chopped fresh thyme or
1 teaspoon dried thyme

1 Heat oil in a frying pan over a medium heat, add leeks and cook, turning frequently, for 5 minutes or until golden. Add sugar and cook, stirring, for 3 minutes longer.

2 Stir wine and thyme into pan and bring to the boil. Reduce heat and simmer for 5 minutes or until leeks are soft and wine reduces.

Serves 4

Soak leeks in several changes of cold water to ensure that any dirt which may have collected between the leaves is rinsed away. Pat dry with absorbent kitchen paper before cooking.

Fruit with Passion Fruit Custard

FRUIT WITH PASSION FRUIT CUSTARD

Vegetarian

2 quinces, peeled
¹/₂ cup/125 g/4 oz sugar
¹/₄ cup/60 mL/2 fl oz sweet dessert wine
water

PASSION FRUIT CUSTARD
³/₄ cup/185 mL/6 fl oz milk
1 teaspoon vanilla essence
2 egg yolks
¹/₃ cup/90 mL/3 fl oz passion fruit pulp
¹/₂ cup/125 mL/4 fl oz cream (double), whipped

1 Place quinces in a large saucepan. Add sugar, wine and enough water to cover. Bring to the boil, then reduce heat and simmer for 3 hours or until quinces are tender and a rich pink colour.

2 To make custard, place milk and vanilla essence in a saucepan and heat over a medium heat until almost boiling. Whisk in egg yolks and cook, stirring, until mixture thickens. Remove pan from heat and set aside to cool. Fold passion fruit pulp and cream into custard.

3 To serve, cut quinces into quarters and serve with custard.

Serves 4

When quinces are unavailable peaches, nectarines or pears are all delicious alternatives. Just remember most other fruit will only require 15-30 minutes cooking.
The Passion Fruit Custard is delicious served with any poached fruit. If fresh passion fruit is not available, canned passion fruit pulp may be used instead.

KNOWING YOUR INGREDIENTS

Beans, peas, lentils and rice appear as staple ingredients throughout this book. In many recipes, canned beans have been used, to save time, however it is not as economic as using the dried product.

In all recipes where canned beans are used, cooked dried beans can be used instead if you wish – just remember you will need to allow soaking and cooking time.

LEGUMES

It is the dried seeds or beans of the plants from the *Leguminosae* family that are referred to as legumes or pulses; namely dried peas, beans and lentils. These foods should play an important role in everyone's diet. However for vegetarians and semi-vegetarians, they are even more important as they are one of the major sources of protein.

Preparing legumes: All legumes except lentils and split peas require soaking before cooking. Soaking helps to clean and soften them. Soaking lentils and split peas will speed up the cooking time. Depending on how much time is available, legumes can have either a long or short soak.

Long soak: This method of preparation requires a little forethought. To prepare legumes, rinse, then place in a large bowl. Cover with cold water, then cover the bowl and set aside to soak overnight at room temperature.

If soaking lentils or split peas, only 10-15 minutes is required. Drain and replace water before cooking.

Short soak: For this method, simply place the legumes in a large saucepan, cover with water and bring to the boil. Reduce heat and simmer for 5 minutes. Remove the pan from the heat and set aside to soak for 1-2 hours. Drain and rinse before using.

Cooking legumes: The cooking time depends on the type, age and quality of the beans. The fresher the beans, the shorter the cooking time. Place legumes in a large saucepan and add enough cold water to cover them by 5 cm/2 in. Do not add salt to the cooking water as this causes the skin to split and the inside to toughen. (If you need to add salt, taste the completed dish towards the end of cooking and correct seasoning as necessary.) Bring to the boil and boil rapidly for at least 5 minutes. Red kidney beans should be boiled for 10-15 minutes to kill the toxins in them. The cooking time for most dried beans varies between 45 minutes and $1^1/2$ hours. The exceptions are adzuki beans which only take 30-45 minutes and soya beans which can take 2-4 hours. Lentils and split peas take 20-30 minutes.

RICE

At least one-third of the human race eats rice as a staple food. There are many varieties and no preparation is required. Cooking varies according to the type of rice and the recipe. Some of the most popular rices are:

Short-grain rice: This is the most popular all-purpose rice and is particularly suited to dishes where grains need to cling together.

Long-grain rice: This rice is characterised by its fluffy texture and is good for pilaus, salads and stuffings.

Brown rice: This natural unpolished rice has a distinctive nutty taste and is highly nutritious. Also available as a quick-cooking product.

Basmati and jasmine rice: Grown in Bangladesh, Pakistan and Thailand these aromatic rices are becoming increasingly popular and are delicious served with highly spiced Indian and Thai dishes.

Arborio or risotto rice: This Italian rice is ideal for absorbing a great deal of liquid and is the best rice for making risotto and jambalaya.

Wild rice: Although related to the rice family, wild rice is actually a seed from an aquatic wild grass which grows in North America. It has an appealing distinctive nutty flavour.

INDEX

ACKNOWLEDGEMENTS

Accoutrement Cookshops
611 Military Road,
Mosman, Sydney
Ph: (02) 969 1031
Shop 507 A,
Carousel Shopping Centre,
Bondi Junction, Sydney
Ph: (02) 387 8468

Art House
64 Elizabeth St
Paddington
Ph: (02) 328 7587

Limoges Australia
Available from David Jones and
Georges (Melbourne)
Ph: (02) 328 6876 enquires